Nutella Cookbook

A Dessert Cookbook Filled with Delicious and Easy Nutella Recipes

By
BookSumo Press
All rights reserved

Published by
http://www.booksumo.com

ENJOY THE RECIPES?
KEEP ON COOKING WITH 6 MORE FREE COOKBOOKS!

Visit our website and simply enter your email address to join the club and receive your 6 cookbooks.

http://booksumo.com/magnet

https://www.instagram.com/booksumopress/

https://www.facebook.com/booksumo/

LEGAL NOTES

All Rights Reserved. No Part Of This Book May Be Reproduced Or Transmitted In Any Form Or By Any Means. Photocopying, Posting Online, And / Or Digital Copying Is Strictly Prohibited Unless Written Permission Is Granted By The Book's Publishing Company. Limited Use Of The Book's Text Is Permitted For Use In Reviews Written For The Public.

Table of Contents

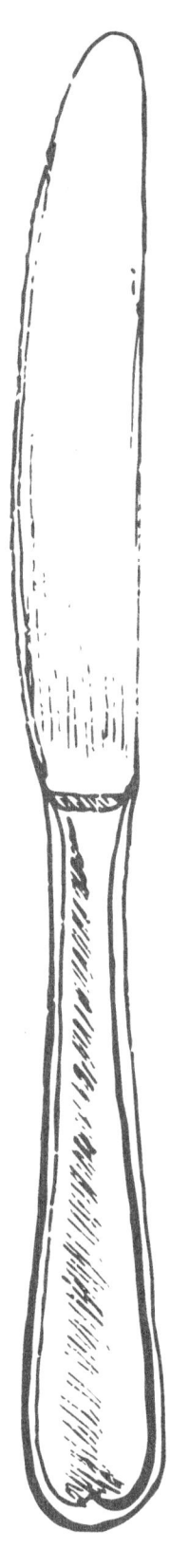

A Pie of Peanut Butter and Nutella 7
Grilled Pineapple Enhanced 8
A Peanut Butter and Chocolate Pie 9
Hazelnut Roll 10
Super Easy Peanut Butter Cups 11
A Pizza Topped with Bananas and Nutella 12
Nutella Chow-Chow 13
Easy Hazelnut Cookies 14
French Toast Enhanced 15
Mug Cake Nutella I 16
Very Easy Nutella Cheesecake 17
Nutella Popsicles 18
Hot Chocolate Enhanced 19
Nutella Cups 20
Mug Cake Nutella II 21
Nutella Ice Pops II 22
Midsummer Nutella Dip 23
Nutella Roll Up 24
Classical Nutella Smoothie 25
Coconut Pops Enhanced 26
Super-Easy Nutella Cookies 27
Enhanced No-Bake Pie 28
Cinnamon Nutella No-Bake Cookies 29
Nutella Smores Done Right 30
Microwave Nutella Cake 31
Graham Crackers Re-Imagined 32
Nutella Frosting 33

Broomstick Dip 34
Chocolate-Cinnamon Dip 35
Banana Cake 36
Peanut Butter Re-Imagined 37
Delightful Nutella Sandwich 38
Nutella Pudding 39
Chocolate Spread II 40
Coffee Enhanced 41
Maggie's Homemade Granola Crisps 42
Toast from France 43
Choco Cookies 44
Hazelnut Puff Pastry Rolls 45
No-Bake Hazelnut Oat Bars 46
Pretzel Cookies 47
Upstate New York Style Crepes 48
Easy Smores 49
Sweet Cookies 50
Maggie's Favorite Hazelnut Cupcakes 51
Truffle and Hazelnut Desserts 52
Pancakes from Denmark 53
Strawberry Hazelnut Bark 54
Two Times Chocolate Cookies 55
Hazelnut Peanut Butter Sandwiches 56
Nutella Puff Pastry 57
5 Minute Hazelnut Topped Donut 58
Australian Hazelnut Pops 59
Australian Hazelnut Crepes 60
Granola New Zealand 61

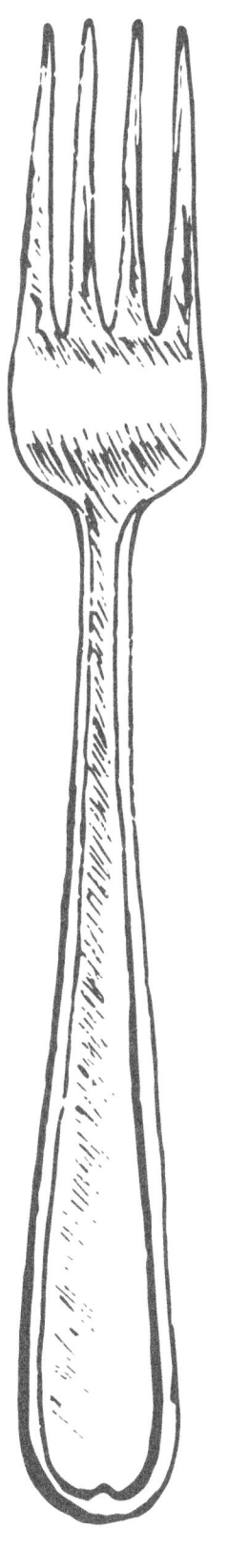

Australian Dream Bars 62
Chocolate Hazelnut Empanadas 63
Hazelnut Snack Sandwiches 64
Rainbow Sandwiches 65
Zara's Sweet Wontons 66
Sweet Wontons New Zealand 67
French Hazelnut and Chocolate Sandwich Cookies 68
Pavlova II 69
Dessert Wontons 70
Nutella Truffles 71
Kid's Favorite Strawberries 73

A Pie of Peanut Butter and Nutella

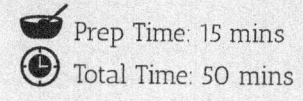

Prep Time: 15 mins
Total Time: 50 mins

Servings per Recipe: 48
Calories	52 kcal
Carbohydrates	5.2 g
Cholesterol	7 mg
Fat	3 g
Protein	1.5 g
Sodium	53 mg

Ingredients

- 8 ounces reduced-fat cream cheese, softened
- 1/2 cup peanut butter
- 1/2 cup chocolate-hazelnut spread (such as Nutella®)
- 1/4 cup agave syrup
- 1/4 cup honey
- 1 egg
- 1 tsp vanilla extract
- 1/2 tsp baking soda
- 1/4 tsp sea salt

Directions

1. At first, preheat your oven to 350 degrees F before doing anything else.
2. Whisk cream cheese, chocolate-hazelnut spread, honey, egg, peanut butter, vanilla extract, baking soda, agave syrup and sea salt in a bowl very thoroughly until you see that a dough is formed.
3. Drop this dough into the baking dish with the help of a spoon.
4. Now bake this in the preheated oven for about 12 minutes.
5. Let it cool for three minutes before serving.
6. Enjoy.

GRILLED Pineapple Enhanced

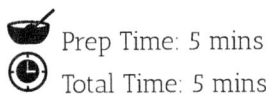

Prep Time: 5 mins
Total Time: 5 mins

Servings per Recipe: 4
Calories	246 kcal
Carbohydrates	28.5 g
Cholesterol	1 mg
Fat	14.3 g
Protein	4 g
Sodium	37 mg

Ingredients

1/2 cup chocolate-hazelnut spread (such as Nutella®)
1/4 cup milk

1/2 fresh pineapple, peeled and cored
1/4 cup walnuts

Directions

1. At first you need to set a grill to medium heat and put some oil before starting anything else.
2. Heat up the mixture of chocolate hazelnut spread and milk in a saucepan until you see that the spread has melted.
3. Cook pineapple on the preheated grill for about 5 minutes on each side before pouring the chocolate mixture over it in a serving dish.
4. Serve.

A Peanut Butter and Chocolate Pie Which Requires No Baking

Prep Time: 15 mins
Total Time: 4 hrs 30 mins

Servings per Recipe: 4
Calories	894 kcal
Carbohydrates	60.7 g
Cholesterol	121 mg
Fat	68.7 g
Protein	15.7 g
Sodium	505 mg

Ingredients

3/4 cup chocolate-hazelnut spread (such as Nutella®)
1 (9 inch) prepared graham cracker crust
1 3/4 cups heavy whipping cream
3/4 cup peanut butter
1/2 cup cream cheese, softened
1/4 cup sweetened condensed milk

Directions

1. Refrigerate graham cracker crust for about 30 minutes after spreading chocolate hazelnut over it.
2. With the help of an electric mixer, beat cream until you see that the required smoothness is achieved before transferring it to a bowl and setting it aside for later use.
3. Whish peanut butter, condensed milk and cream cheese together in a bowl until you see that the required smoothness is achieved before adding the remaining whipped cream.
4. Also add some whipped cream over it before refrigerating it for at least four full hours.

HAZELNUT Roll

Prep Time: 45 mins
Total Time: 1 hr 10 mins

Servings per Recipe: 12
Calories   350 kcal
Carbohydrates   44.8 g
Cholesterol   32 mg
Fat   16.1 g
Protein   7.7 g
Sodium   367 mg

Ingredients

Rolls:
3 cups bread flour
1 cup milk
5 tbsps white sugar
1/4 cup butter, melted
1 egg
2 1/4 tsps instant yeast
1 1/2 tsps salt

Filling:
2 tbsps butter, softened
1 cup chocolate-hazelnut spread (such as Nutella®)
1/2 cup coarsely chopped hazelnuts

Directions

1. At first, preheat your oven to 350 degrees F before doing anything else.
2. Add a mixture of bread flour, salt, milk, melted butter, yeast, white sugar and eggs into the bread machine, and start it after selecting the dough cycle.
3. Roll this dough over a floured surface into large sized rectangles before adding butter and chocolate hazelnut spread over it.
4. Add some hazelnuts and then roll it around the filling before cutting into 12 even sized parts.
5. Place them in the baking dish.
6. Now bake this in the preheated oven for about 25 minutes.

Super Easy Peanut Butter Cups

Prep Time: 15 mins
Total Time: 1 hr 15 mins

Servings per Recipe: 4
Calories	231 kcal
Carbohydrates	13.7 g
Cholesterol	0 mg
Fat	19.1 g
Protein	5.4 g
Sodium	91 mg

Ingredients

Peanut Butter Layer:
3/4 cup peanut butter
2 tbsps coconut oil, melted
1 tbsp raw honey
Chocolate Layer:
1/2 cup chocolate-hazelnut spread (such as Nutella®), or more to taste

1/4 cup raw cocoa powder
1/4 cup coconut oil, melted
1 tbsp raw honey
1 tbsp peanut butter
1 packet stevia powder

Directions

1. Mix 3/4 cup peanut butter, 1 tbsp honey and 2 tbsps coconut oil in a medium sized bowl, and in a separate bowl, combine chocolate hazelnut spread, 1/4 cup coconut oil, 1 tbsp honey, 1 tbsp peanut butter, cocoa powder and stevia powder.
2. Pour peanut butter mixture into muffin cups of your choice before topping each cup with the chocolate mixture.
3. Refrigerate or freeze before serving.

A PIZZA
Topped with Bananas and Nutella

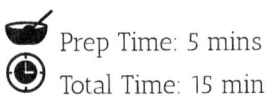

Prep Time: 5 mins
Total Time: 15 mins

Servings per Recipe: 4
Calories	249 kcal
Carbohydrates	36 g
Cholesterol	0 mg
Fat	10.6 g
Protein	4 g
Sodium	158 mg

Ingredients

1/2 cup chocolate-hazelnut spread (such as Nutella®), or to taste
1 large tortilla

1 banana, cut into 1/4-inch-thick slices

Directions

1. Put hazelnut chocolate spread over a tortilla evenly before spreading banana slices on top of it.
2. Cook tortilla over high heat for about 5 minutes or until you see that it is crispy.
3. Allow it to cool for four minutes before cutting it into four equal slices.
4. Serve.

Nutella Chow-Chow

Prep Time: 10 mins
Total Time: 15 mins

Servings per Recipe: 8
Calories   233 kcal
Carbohydrates   41.4 g
Cholesterol   0 mg
Fat   8.3 g
Protein   2.3 g
Sodium   150 mg

Ingredients

- 1 (11 ounce) package milk chocolate chips
- 1/2 cup chocolate-hazelnut spread (such as Nutella®)
- 8 cups bite-size corn square cereal (such as Corn Chex®)
- 1 1/2 cups confectioners' sugar

Directions

1. Melt down a mixture of chocolate hazelnut spread and chocolate chips over high heat before adding cereal and mixing it thoroughly.
2. Now transfer this cereal mixture to a bag and shake it well after adding confectioners' sugar into it.
3. Transfer this chow-chow to a container that is airtight.
4. Enjoy your chow-chow.
5. NOTE: Chow-chow should be thought of as a popcorn replacement.

EASY
Hazelnut Cookies

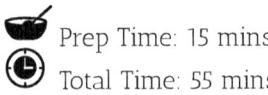
Prep Time: 15 mins
Total Time: 55 mins

Servings per Recipe: 12
Calories	237 kcal
Carbohydrates	22.3 g
Cholesterol	0 mg
Fat	15.6 g
Protein	3.3 g
Sodium	70 mg

Ingredients

1 sheet frozen puff pastry, thawed
1 cup chocolate-hazelnut spread (such as Nutella®)
1/3 cup finely chopped, roasted hazelnuts

Directions

1. Put chocolate hazelnut spread and hazelnuts evenly over puff pastry.
2. Take the long edge and roll it around the filling until you reach the middle, and do the same with the other long edge to meet the first roll in the middle.
3. Refrigerate it for at least thirty minutes before you do anything else.
4. Set your oven at 450 degrees F.
5. Take out the pastry and cut it into slices that are ¾ inch approx.
6. Put these slices in the preheated oven over baking sheet and bake it for 7 minutes before turning it and baking it for another 5 minutes.
7. Serve.

French Toast Enhanced

Prep Time: 15 mins
Total Time: 25 mins

Servings per Recipe: 2
Calories   563 kcal
Carbohydrates   63.1 g
Cholesterol   219 mg
Fat   28 g
Protein   13.9 g
Sodium   552 mg

Ingredients

1/4 cup chocolate-hazelnut spread (such as Nutella®)
4 slices bread
1 banana, sliced
1/4 cup chocolate milk
2 eggs, beaten
1 tbsp vanilla extract
1/2 tsp ground cinnamon
2 tbsps butter

Directions

1. Put chocolate hazelnut spread on one side of two bread slices before topping them with banana slices.
2. Place the remaining bread slices on top to form two sandwiches.
3. Mix cinnamon, chocolate milk, vanilla extract and eggs in a medium sized bowl and dip those sandwiches in it completely to get completely coated.
4. Cook these sandwiches over low heat in hot butter for about 6 minutes each side.
5. Serve.

MUG CAKE
Nutella I

Prep Time: 5 mins
Total Time: 12 mins

Servings per Recipe: 1
Calories	450 kcal
Carbohydrates	65.8 g
Cholesterol	0 mg
Fat	18 g
Protein	9.9 g
Sodium	203 mg

Ingredients

2 tbsps all-purpose flour
2 tbsps coconut flour
1 tbsp cocoa powder
1/4 tsp baking powder
3 1/2 tbsps almond milk, divided

1/2 tsp vanilla extract
3 tbsps chocolate-hazelnut spread (such as Nutella®)

Directions

1. Combine coconut flour, cocoa powder, all-purpose flour and baking powder in a medium sized bowl before adding 3 tbsps almond milk, Nutella®, vanilla extract and 1/2 tbsp milk one by one into the flour mixture, while stirring continuously in that time.
2. Pour this mixture into a mug and cook this in the microwave for about one minutes before letting it stand as it is for five seconds and cooking it again for 30 seconds more in the microwave oven.
3. Let it cool before serving.

Very Easy Nutella Cheesecake

Prep Time: 10 mins
Total Time: 4 hrs 10 mins

Servings per Recipe: 8
Calories   627 kcal
Carbohydrates   61.4 g
Cholesterol   62 mg
Fat   40.2 g
Protein   8.4 g
Sodium   380 mg

Ingredients

2 (8 ounce) packages cream cheese, room temperature
1/2 cup white sugar
1 (13 ounce) jar chocolate-hazelnut spread, such as Nutella
1/4 tsp vanilla extract
1 (9 inch) prepared graham cracker crust

Directions

1. Take out a large bowl and mix cream, sugar, Nutella and vanilla before putting it in a freezer for about 4 hours.
2. Serve.

NUTELLA
Popsicles

Prep Time: 10 mins
Total Time: 3 hrs 15 mins

Servings per Recipe: 8
Calories   281 kcal
Carbohydrates   10.2 g
Cholesterol   62 mg
Fat   40.2 g
Protein   84 g
Sodium   24 mg

Ingredients

6 tbsps chocolate-hazelnut spread (such as Nutella)
1 cup milk
2 cups heavy whipping cream

Directions

1. Mix cream, chocolate hazelnut and milk together in a bowl before putting it in the microwave oven for 2 minutes to melt down the hazelnut while stirring every 30 seconds.
2. Pour this mixture in ice pop molds and freeze it for about 4 hours.

Hot Chocolate Enhanced

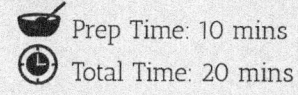

Prep Time: 10 mins
Total Time: 20 mins

Servings per Recipe: 8
Calories	627 kcal
Carbohydrates	61.4 g
Cholesterol	62 mg
Fat	40.2 g
Protein	8.4 g
Sodium	380 mg

Ingredients

3/4 cup hazelnut liqueur (such as Frangelico)
1 (13 ounce) jar chocolate-hazelnut spread (such as Nutella)
1 quart half-and-half

Directions

1. Put half and half to low heat in a saucepan and add chocolate hazelnut spread.
2. Cook for about 10 minutes and just before serving add hazelnut liqueur.

NUTELLA
Cups

Prep Time: 10 mins
Total Time: 20 mins

Servings per Recipe: 12
Calories	245 kcal
Carbohydrates	28.9 g
Cholesterol	0 mg
Fat	12.6 g
Protein	3.9 g
Sodium	309 mg

Ingredients

2 (8 ounce) packages refrigerated crescent rolls
2 ripe bananas, sliced
12 tbsps chocolate-hazelnut spread (such as Nutella), or more to taste

1 tsp confectioners' sugar, or to taste

Directions

1. First, preheat your oven to 375 degrees before continuing.
2. Put 2 crescent roll triangles into muffin cups and fill these cups with banana slices and chocolate hazelnut over the banana slices.
3. Now bake this for about 13 minutes or until golden brown and serve.

Mug Cake
Nutella II

Prep Time: 10 mins
Total Time: 13 mins

Servings per Recipe: 12
Calories 475 kcal
Carbohydrates 113g
Cholesterol 190 mg
Fat 62.8 g
Protein 17.1 g
Sodium 534 mg

Ingredients

1/4 cup self-rising flour
1/4 cup white sugar
1 egg, beaten
3 tbsps cocoa powder
3 tbsps chocolate-hazelnut spread (such as Nutella)
3 tbsps milk
3 tbsps vegetable oil

Directions

1. Mix all the ingredients mentioned in a coffee mug with a fork until you find it smooth.
2. Cook this in the microwave oven for about 3 minutes.
3. Enjoy.

NUTELLA
Ice Pops II

Prep Time: 10 mins
Total Time: 3 hrs 10 mins

Servings per Recipe: 8
Calories	137 kcal
Carbohydrates	12.8g
Cholesterol	14 mg
Fat	8.8 g
Protein	2.5 g
Sodium	47 mg

Ingredients

1 cup whipped cream
1/2 cup whole milk
1/4 cup chocolate-hazelnut spread
(such as Nutella)

Directions

1. Put all the ingredients mentioned into a blender and blend it for about 2 minutes.
2. Now pour this mixture into ice pop molds and place them in your freezer for about 3 hours to get solid.

Midsummer Nutella Dip

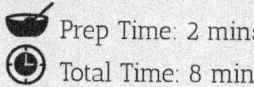

Prep Time: 2 mins
Total Time: 8 mins

Servings per Recipe: 4
Calories	110 kcal
Carbohydrates	13.8g
Cholesterol	< 1 mg
Fat	5.8 g
Protein	1.5 g
Sodium	22 mg

Ingredients

5 tbsps chocolate-hazelnut spread (such as Nutella)
2 tbsps milk
1 tsp honey
1/4 tsp vanilla extract

Directions

1. Mix all the ingredients mentioned and put them to heat in the microwave for about 1 minute.
2. Let it cool for 2 minutes before serving.

NUTELLA
Roll Up

🥣 Prep Time: 5 mins
🕐 Total Time: 5 mins

Servings per Recipe: 2
Calories   317 kcal
Carbohydrates   49 g
Cholesterol   0 mg
Fat   11.9 g
Protein   5.5 g
Sodium   259 mg

Ingredients

1 tortilla
1/4 cup chocolate-hazelnut spread
(such as Nutella)

1 small banana

Directions

1. Put chocolate spread on the corners of a tortilla that is warmed in the microwave oven for 10 seconds and fold it around the banana slice.
2. Cut it into half and serve.

Classical Nutella Smoothie

Prep Time: 10 mins
Total Time: 10 mins

Servings per Recipe: 1
Calories   457 kcal
Carbohydrates   67.4g
Cholesterol   7 mg
Fat   11.4 g
Protein   24.9 g
Sodium   190 mg

Ingredients

- 6 fluid ounces low-fat milk
- 6 ounces plain fat-free Greek yogurt
- 1 banana, sliced
- 4 fresh strawberries
- 2 tbsps chocolate-hazelnut spread (such as Nutella)

Directions

1. Put all the ingredients mentioned into blender and blend until smooth.

COCONUT POPS
Enhanced

 Prep Time: 5 mins
Total Time: 4 hrs 5 mins

Servings per Recipe: 6
Calories 340 kcal
Carbohydrates 47.4g
Cholesterol 0 mg
Fat 16.6 g
Protein 2.1 g
Sodium 44 mg

Ingredients

1 (14 ounce) can coconut cream
1/2 cup chocolate-hazelnut spread
(such as Nutella), or more to taste

Directions

1. Whisk coconut cream until smooth and add chocolate hazelnut spread and mix it well.
2. Pour this mixture into ice-pop molds and let it freeze for about 4 hours.
3. Serve

Super-Easy Nutella Cookies

Prep Time: 10 mins
Total Time: 30 mins

Servings per Recipe: 6
Calories   169 kcal
Carbohydrates   26.5g
Cholesterol   62 mg
Fat   4.9 g
Protein   4.9 g
Sodium   34 mg

Ingredients

- 1 cup all-purpose flour
- 2 tbsps white sugar
- 2 eggs
- 1/4 cup chocolate-hazelnut spread (such as Nutella)

Directions

1. First, preheat your oven to 350 degrees F before continuing.
2. Combine flour and sugar together in a medium sized bowl and add eggs and mix thoroughly.
3. Now add chocolate hazelnut spread and place into a baking sheet by making several balls and pressing them.
4. Bake this in the preheated oven for about 25 minutes.
5. Let it cool down and serve.

ENHANCED
No-Bake Pie

🥣 Prep Time: 10 mins
🕐 Total Time: 4 hrs 20 mins

Servings per Recipe: 6
Calories   759 kcal
Carbohydrates   72.8g
Cholesterol   41 mg
Fat   50 g
Protein   8.9 g
Sodium   406 mg

Ingredients

1 (13 ounce) jar chocolate-hazelnut spread (such as Nutella), divided
1 (9 inch) prepared graham cracker crust
1 (8 ounce) package cream cheese, softened
1 (8 ounce) container frozen whipped topping, thawed

Directions

1. Put a quarter cup of chocolate hazelnut spread over graham cracker crust.
2. Now whisk hazelnut spread and some cream cheese in some bowl until you find it smooth and add whipped topping before putting this mixture over the crust.
3. Put the mixture in the refrigerator for about 4 hours.
4. Enjoy.

Cinnamon Nutella No-Bake Cookies

🥣 Prep Time: 10 mins
🕐 Total Time: 15 mins

Servings per Recipe: 6
Calories   152 kcal
Carbohydrates   22.7g
Cholesterol   7 mg
Fat   22.7g
Protein   1.9 g
Sodium   40 mg

Ingredients

2 cups white sugar
1/2 cup butter
1/2 cup milk
1 (10 ounce) package cinnamon chips
1/2 cup chocolate-hazelnut spread (such as Nutella)
3 cups old-fashioned rolled oats

Directions

1. Put some parchment paper over a baking sheet and mix sugar, milk, and butter in a small saucepan and cook for about 2 minutes.
2. After removing this saucepan from the heat, add cinnamon chips, hazelnut spread, and some oats.
3. Now place a cookie sized mixture into a baking sheet and allow it to cool down.
4. Serve.

NUTELLA
Smores Done Right

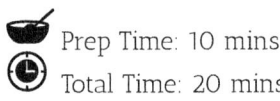
Prep Time: 10 mins
Total Time: 20 mins

Servings per Recipe:	4
Calories	79 kcal
Carbohydrates	12.5g
Cholesterol	0 mg
Fat	3 g
Protein	1 g
Sodium	52 mg

Ingredients

4 whole graham crackers, broken into two square halves
2 tbsps chocolate-hazelnut spread (such as Nutella)
2 tbsps marshmallow cream

Directions

1. Put half a tsp of hazelnut spread over four graham cracker halves and half tsp marshmallow cream over the remaining 3 cracker halves.
2. Now take one marshmallow half, and one hazelnut spread topped half, and press together.
3. Do this for all crackers to get multiple sets and serve.

Microwave Nutella Cake

⏲ Prep Time: 10 mins
🕐 Total Time: 15 mins

Servings per Recipe: 2
Calories   475 kcal
Carbohydrates   50.4g
Cholesterol   95 mg
Fat   28.8 g
Protein   7.5 g
Sodium   840 mg

Ingredients

1/4 cup self-rising flour
1/4 cup white sugar
1 egg
3 tbsps vegetable oil
3 tbsps milk
2 tbsps unsweetened cocoa powder, or more to taste
2 tbsps chocolate-hazelnut spread (such as Nutella), or more to taste
1/2 tsp salt
1/2 tsp vanilla extract

Directions

1. Put all the ingredients mentioned into a large sized mug and whisk it until smooth.
2. Now cook this in a microwave oven for about 2 minutes or until the cake has risen.
3. Serve.

GRAHAM CRACKERS
Re-Imagined

Prep Time: 20 mins
Total Time: 20 mins

Servings per Recipe: 30
Calories	144 kcal
Carbohydrates	20.3g
Cholesterol	5 mg
Fat	6.4 g
Protein	2.1 g
Sodium	103 mg

Ingredients

30 sliced fresh strawberries
1 (7 ounce) can whipped cream
1 (13 ounce) jar chocolate-hazelnut spread (such as Nutella)
30 fresh blueberries
1 (14.4 ounce) package mini graham crackers

Directions

1. First, cut the bottom part of each strawberry and create a hole in each of them from the top.
2. Now put whipped cream and hazelnut spread into this hole, and top this with one blueberry.
3. Cover with a graham cracker before serving.
4. Enjoy.

Nutella Frosting

Prep Time: 5 mins
Total Time: 5 mins

Servings per Recipe: 22
Calories   144 kcal
Carbohydrates   20.3g
Cholesterol   0 mg
Fat   6.4 g
Protein   2.1 g
Sodium   103 mg

Ingredients

1 (16 ounce) can prepared chocolate frosting
3/4 cup chocolate-hazelnut spread (such as Nutella)
3/4 cup confectioners' sugar
1 tsp vanilla extract

Directions

1. Put all the ingredients mentioned into a blender and blend for about 2 minutes or until smooth.
2. Serve.
3. NOTE: Use as a topping for cakes, cookies, and even tortillas.

BROOMSTICK
Dip

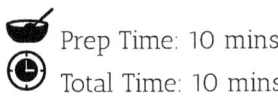

Prep Time: 10 mins
Total Time: 10 mins

Servings per Recipe: 16
Calories	291 kcal
Carbohydrates	36 g
Cholesterol	0 mg
Fat	13.7 g
Protein	8.2 g
Sodium	707 mg

Ingredients

1 cup smooth peanut butter
1 cup chocolate-hazelnut spread (such as Nutella)
1 (16 ounce) bag small pretzel rods
1/2 cup oatmeal cereal squares (such as Quaker Oatmeal Squares), crushed

Directions

1. Combine peanut butter and hazelnut spread thoroughly in serving bowl and add some crushed cereal squares.
2. Now take out pretzel rods and dip them into this mixture to get broomsticks.
3. Plate and enjoy.

Chocolate-Cinnamon Dip

Prep Time: 10 mins
Total Time: 1 hr 10 mins

Servings per Recipe: 6
Calories   90 kcal
Carbohydrates   8.8g
Cholesterol   8 mg
Fat   5.8 g
Protein   0.8 g
Sodium   31 mg

Ingredients

1 (8 ounce) package cream cheese, softened
1 (7 ounce) jar marshmallow creme
1 (12 ounce) container frozen whipped topping, thawed
1 tsp ground cinnamon
1/2 tsp vanilla extract
2 1/2 tbsps chocolate-hazelnut spread, such as Nutella

Directions

1. Take out a large bowl and mix cream cheese, whipped topping and marshmallow cream in a blender.
2. Now add cinnamon, chocolate spread and vanilla and continuing mixing.
3. Cover this dip with plastic wrap in a serving dish before refrigerating for one hour.
4. Enjoy.

BANANA
Cake

Prep Time: 10 mins
Total Time: 12 mins

Servings per Recipe: 2
Calories	493 kcal
Carbohydrates	62.2g
Cholesterol	2 mg
Fat	25.9 g
Protein	5.2 g
Sodium	57 mg

Ingredients

6 tbsps whole wheat flour
4 1/2 tbsps white sugar
1/8 tsp baking powder
1/2 banana, mashed
3 tbsps milk

3 tbsps vegetable oil
1 1/2 tsps vanilla extract
2 tbsps chocolate-hazelnut spread (such as Nutella), or to taste (optional)

Directions

1. Mix flour, sugar, and baking powder together in a bowl. Stir banana, milk, oil, and vanilla extract together in a microwave-safe bowl; stir in flour mixture until batter is smooth.
2. Cook in microwave until cake is cooked through, about 2 minutes. Cool slightly and spread chocolate-hazelnut spread onto cake.

Peanut Butter Re-Imagined

Prep Time: 5 mins
Total Time: 40 mins

Servings per Recipe: 15
Calories	186 kcal
Carbohydrates	28g
Cholesterol	9 mg
Fat	7.8 g
Protein	3.6 g
Sodium	56 mg

Ingredients

1 (14 ounce) can sweetened condensed milk
1/4 cup creamy peanut butter
1/4 cup hazelnut-flavored syrup for beverages
2 tbsps honey
1 tsp vanilla extract
1 cup chocolate chips

Directions

1. Put all the ingredients except chocolate chips that are mentioned into saucepan and mix it thoroughly before cooking it at medium heat for about 5 minutes.
2. Remove this saucepan from the heat and add chocolate chips while stirring regularly to get it melted.
3. Pour this into some jar and let it cool down.
4. NOTE: Use this mixture as a peanut butter replacement.

DELIGHTFUL
Nutella Sandwich

Prep Time: 10 mins
Total Time: 20 mins

Servings per Recipe: 11
Calories   473 kcal
Carbohydrates   52.3g
Cholesterol   0 mg
Fat   25.8 g
Protein   13.4 g
Sodium   378 mg

Ingredients

2 tbsps almond butter
2 slices multigrain bread
1 tbsp chocolate hazelnut spread

1/2 bananas, sliced

Directions

1. Place bananas over the almond butter that is spread over 1 side of one slice and place this over the other slice of the bread which also has chocolate spread topping to make a delicious sandwich.

Nutella Pudding

Prep Time: 10 mins
Total Time: 40 mins

Servings per Recipe: 2
Calories	459 kcal
Carbohydrates	26.2g
Cholesterol	41 mg
Fat	31.7 g
Protein	30 g
Sodium	209 mg

Ingredients

- 1/2 cup skinned hazelnuts
- 1 cup low-fat ricotta cheese
- 3 tbsps cocoa powder (such as Callebaut)
- 2 tbsps stevia powder
- 1/2 scoop vanilla whey protein powder
- 1 tsp vanilla extract

Directions

1. First, preheat your oven to 375 degrees and spread hazelnuts on a baking sheet before continuing.
2. Now place this baking sheet into the microwave oven for about 12 minutes and let it cool down.
3. Now put hazelnuts, stevia, ricotta, cocoa power, vanilla protein powder and vanilla in the blender and blend until smooth.

CHOCOLATE
Spread II

Prep Time: 10 mins
Total Time: 10 mins

Servings per Recipe: 12
Calories	155 kcal
Carbohydrates	5.1g
Cholesterol	41 mg
Fat	15.5 g
Protein	0.4 g
Sodium	3 mg

Ingredients

- 1 cup unsalted butter, softened
- 3 tbsps honey, or more to taste
- 3 tbsps unsweetened cocoa powder

Directions

1. Whisk butter and honey very thoroughly until both are completely mixed and add cocoa mix it well
2. You can store this in the refrigerator for two weeks.

Coffee
Enhanced

Prep Time: 10 mins
Total Time: 10 mins

Servings per Recipe: 2
Calories   267 kcal
Carbohydrates   38.3g
Cholesterol   15 mg
Fat   8.1 g
Protein   7.3 g
Sodium   99 mg

Ingredients

2 cups ice cubes
1 1/2 cups milk
3 tbsps white sugar
2 tbsps chocolate-hazelnut spread (such as Nutella)

4 tsps instant coffee granules
1 tbsp vanilla extract

Directions

1. Put all the ingredients mentioned into a blender and blend for about 30 seconds or until the required smoothness is achieved.
2. Enjoy your unique tasting coffee.

MAGGIE'S Homemade Granola Crisps

Prep Time: 15 mins
Total Time: 1 hr 30 mins

Servings per Recipe: 24
Calories	150 kcal
Fat	2.8 g
Carbohydrates	29.8g
Protein	2.5 g
Cholesterol	0 mg
Sodium	108 mg

Ingredients

1 C. raisins (optional)
3/4 C. unsweetened applesauce
3 tbsps unsweetened applesauce
2/3 C. chocolate-hazelnut spread
1/2 C. brown sugar
1/4 C. honey
2 tbsps corn syrup

2 tbsps vanilla extract
1 tbsp ground cinnamon
1 tbsp salt
3 1/3 C. old-fashioned oats
2/3 C. all-purpose flour

Directions

1. Coat a casserole dish with oil and then set your oven to 350 degrees before doing anything else.
2. Get a bowl, combine: salt, raisins, 3/4 C. and 3 tbsps of applesauce, cinnamon, hazelnut spread, vanilla, brown sugar, corn syrup, and honey. Stir the mix until it is even and smooth.
3. Get a 2nd bowl, mix: flour and oats.
4. Combine both bowls and stir the contents. Now add in the granola. Then pour the mix into your casserole dish.
5. Cook everything in the oven for 17 mins then let the contents cool on a rack before slicing the dessert into bars of your preferred size.
6. Enjoy.

Toast from France

Prep Time: 10 mins
Total Time: 15 mins

Servings per Recipe: 2
Calories	296 kcal
Fat	12.8 g
Carbohydrates	39.6g
Protein	11.2 g
Cholesterol	95 mg
Sodium	296 mg

Ingredients

- 2 tbsps chocolate-hazelnut spread, or more to taste
- 4 slices cinnamon bread (such as Pepperidge Farm(R))
- 1/4 C. milk
- 1 large egg, beaten
- 1/4 tbsp vanilla extract
- cooking spray

Directions

1. Coat 1 side of 2 pieces of bread with hazelnut spread. Then form sandwiches with the rest of the bread.
2. Get a bowl, combine: vanilla, milk, and eggs. Submerge each sandwich in this mix for about 20 secs then flip the sandwich and let it sit in the mix for 20 more secs.
3. Coat a skillet with nonstick spray, liberally, then for 3 mins fry the sandwiches in the skillet.
4. After 2 mins of frying flip the sandwich and cook the opposite side for 1 additional min.
5. Enjoy.

CHOCO
Cookies

Prep Time: 30 mins
Total Time: 57 mins

Servings per Recipe: 12
Calories 502 kcal
Fat 26.7 g
Carbohydrates 63.1g
Protein 6.1 g
Cholesterol 68 mg
Sodium 434 mg

Ingredients

2 1/2 C. all-purpose flour
1/4 C. unsweetened cocoa powder
1 tbsp baking soda
1 tbsp salt
1 C. butter, room temperature
3/4 C. brown sugar
3/4 C. white sugar

2 large eggs
2 tbsps vanilla extract
1/2 C. chocolate-hazelnut spread
1/2 C. diced toasted hazelnuts
1 C. chocolate chips

Directions

1. Coat a cookie sheet with oil then set your oven to 350 degrees before doing anything else.
2. Get a bowl, combine: salt, flour, baking soda, and cocoa powder. Mix this evenly until it is completely smooth.
3. Get a 2nd bowl, and with a mixer, combine: white sugar, butter, and brown sugar. Then one by one add in your eggs and continue mixing.
4. After all of the eggs have been combined in add the hazelnut spread and the vanilla. Then stir the mix a few more times.
5. Now gradually combine both bowls and add in the chocolate ships and the hazelnuts.
6. Drop dollops of this mix on the prepared cookie sheet.
7. Cook the cookies in the oven for 14 mins then let them cool on a rack for 5 mins before serving.
8. Enjoy.

Hazelnut Puff Pastry Rolls

Prep Time: 1 hr 10 mins
Total Time: 1 hr 10 mins

Servings per Recipe: 25
Calories   97 kcal
Fat   6.3 g
Carbohydrates   9.2g
Protein   1.1 g
Cholesterol   10 mg
Sodium   76 mg

Ingredients

1 (8 oz.) package phyllo dough, thawed if frozen
1/2 C. melted butter

1/2 (13 oz.) jar chocolate-hazelnut spread

Directions

1. Set your oven to 400 degrees before doing anything else.
2. Take one piece of phyllo and coat half of it with butter then fold the opposite side over the buttered side.
3. Add 1 tbsp of hazelnut spread in the center of the dough then place the rest of the butter around the rest of the dough's surface.
4. Now roll this dough into a tube and layer it on a cookie sheet.
5. Continue preparing the dough pieces in this manner until all the ingredients have been used up.
6. Now cook them in the oven for 12 mins.
7. Enjoy.

NO-BAKE
Hazelnut Oat Bars

Prep Time: 10 mins
Total Time: 50 mins

Servings per Recipe: 30
Calories	230 kcal
Fat	13.4 g
Carbohydrates	25.6 g
Protein	3.8 g
Cholesterol	16 mg
Sodium	111 mg

Ingredients

- 1 C. butter
- 2 C. white sugar
- 1 tbsp vanilla extract
- 1/4 tbsp salt
- 1 C. peanut butter
- 1 C. chocolate-hazelnut spread
- 3 C. rolled oats

Directions

1. Cover a casserole dish with foil before doing anything else.
2. Now begin to heat and stir the following until it is all boiling: salt, butter, vanilla, and sugar.
3. Once the mix is boiling continue heating and stirring for 60 secs.
4. Now lower the heat to a medium level and combine in the hazelnut spread and the peanut butter.
5. Continue heating and stirring for 6 mins then shut the heat and add in your oats.
6. Stir the oats into the mix and pour everything into your casserole dish.
7. Evenly layer the mix throughout the casserole dish with a spoon.
8. Now let the mix set for 40 mins.
9. Remove the foil from the casserole dish and slice the oat mix into bars of your preferred sized.
10. Enjoy.

Pretzel Cookies

Prep Time: 15 mins
Total Time: 35 mins

Servings per Recipe: 26
Calories   239 kcal
Fat   6.2 g
Carbohydrates   41.8g
Protein   4.6 g
Cholesterol   24 mg
Sodium   604 mg

Ingredients

- 2 C. all-purpose flour
- 2 tbsps all-purpose flour
- 1/2 tbsp baking soda
- 1/2 tbsp salt
- 1 C. brown sugar
- 1/2 C. unsalted butter, melted and cooled slightly
- 1 egg
- 1 egg yolk
- 2 tbsps natural peanut butter (such as Natural Jif(R))
- 2 tbsps vanilla extract
- 53 pretzel sticks, crushed
- 3 tbsps chocolate-hazelnut spread

Directions

1. Set your oven to 350 degrees before doing anything else.
2. Get a bowl, combine: salt, 2 C. and 2 tbsps of flour, and baking soda.
3. Get a 2nd bowl, combine: butter and sugar.
4. Then add in vanilla, eggs, peanut butter, and egg yolks.
5. Now combine both bowls gradually, then add the hazelnut spread and the pretzels.
6. Grab two spoons and drop dollops of the mix onto a cookie sheet and cook everything in the oven for 10 mins.
7. Spin your cookie sheet and cook the cookies for 6 more mins.
8. Now let the cookies cool on a rack for 10 mins.
9. Enjoy.

UPSTATE New York Style Crepes

Prep Time: 30 mins
Total Time: 1 hr 15 mins

Servings per Recipe: 12
Calories	406 kcal
Fat	22.8 g
Carbohydrates	40.3g
Protein	13.3 g
Cholesterol	84 mg
Sodium	362 mg

Ingredients

- 1 C. milk
- 4 large eggs
- 1 tbsp butter, melted
- 1 tbsp white sugar
- 1 tbsp almond extract
- 1 1/4 C. all-purpose flour
- 12 slices bacon
- 3 tbsps butter, or as needed - divided
- 6 firm bananas, sliced in half lengthwise
- 12 tbsps chocolate-hazelnut spread, divided
- 12 tbsps peanut butter, divided
- 1/2 tbsp honey, divided
- 1 tbsp confectioners' sugar for dusting, or as needed
- 1 tbsp chocolate syrup, or as needed

Directions

1. Process the following with a blender or food processor until smooth: flour, milk, almond extract, 1 tbsp butter, and white sugar.
2. Let this mix sit for 25 mins then begin to fry your bacon, until crispy, for 12 mins then remove the excess oils. Now melt 1 tbsp of butter in a large frying pan and begin to fry 1/4 C. of batter for 3 mins then jiggle the pan and flip the crepe.
3. Fry the opposite for 2 mins then place the crepe on a plate. Continue cooking crepes in this manner and add more butter to the pan to keep it coated.
4. Once all your crepes are cooked add 2 more tbsp of butter to the pan and begin to fry your banana, until browned, for about 3 to 4 mins per side.
5. Plate one crepe for serving and top it with 1 tbsp of hazelnut spread, 1 tbsp of peanut butter, 1 piece of bacon in the middle, and a half of a banana.
6. Finally add half a tsp of honey over everything.
7. Top the dish with some confectioner's and some chocolate syrup.
8. Shape the crepe into a cylinder and place it in a casserole dish. Continue forming crepes in this manner until all of the ingredients have been used up. Enjoy.

Easy Smores

Prep Time: 10 mins
Total Time: 15 mins

Servings per Recipe: 2
Calories   494 kcal
Fat   33.2 g
Carbohydrates   40g
Protein   12.2 g
Cholesterol   31 mg
Sodium   395 mg

Ingredients

- 2 tbsps salted butter, softened, divided
- 1 tbsp olive oil, divided
- 4 slices 12-grain bread
- 2 tbsps peanut butter
- 2 tbsps marshmallow crème, or to taste
- 2 tbsps chocolate-hazelnut spread

Directions

1. Coat 1 side of each piece of bread with 1.5 tsp olive oil and 1 tbsp of butter.
2. Now add 1.5 tsps of olive oil and 1 tbsp of butter to a skillet and get it hot.
3. On the non-oiled side of each piece of bread layer the following: hazelnut spread, marshmallow crème, and peanut butter.
4. Form sandwiches with the oil sides facing outwards.
5. Fry your sandwiches for 40 secs per side in the hot pan.
6. Enjoy.

SWEET
Cookies

Prep Time: 15 mins
Total Time: 55 mins

Servings per Recipe: 12
Calories   341 kcal
Fat   13.2 g
Carbohydrates   51.8g
Protein   4.7 g
Cholesterol   51 mg
Sodium   153 mg

Ingredients

1/2 C. unsalted butter at room temperature
3/4 C. chocolate-hazelnut spread
1/2 C. white sugar
2/3 C. packed brown sugar
1 egg
1 egg yolk

1/2 tbsp vanilla extract
2 3/4 C. all-purpose flour
3/4 tbsp baking soda
1/4 tbsp salt

Directions

1. Get a bowl, and combine the following with a mixer: brown sugar, butter, white sugar, and hazelnut spread.
2. Now combine in the egg and add the vanilla and egg yolks.
3. Get a 2nd bowl, combine: salt, flour, and baking soda.
4. Slowly combine both bowls while continuing to stir everything.
5. Shape the dough into a large ball and cover the dough in plastic.
6. Place the ball in a 3rd bowl and put everything in the fridge for 40 mins.
7. Now set your oven to 400 degrees before doing anything else.
8. Take your dough and form it into multiple large balls then place them on a baking sheet and flatten the dough balls.
9. Cook the cookies in the oven for 9 mins then let them cool before serving.
10. Enjoy.

Maggie's Favorite Hazelnut Cupcakes

Prep Time: 25 mins
Total Time: 1 hr 40 mins

Servings per Recipe: 18
Calories	391 kcal
Fat	21.2 g
Carbohydrates	48.8g
Protein	5.8 g
Cholesterol	22 mg
Sodium	316 mg

Ingredients

- 2 C. white sugar
- 1 C. all-purpose flour
- 3/4 C. ground toasted hazelnuts
- 3/4 C. unsweetened cocoa powder
- 1 1/2 tbsps baking powder
- 1 1/2 tbsps baking soda
- 1 tbsp salt
- 2 eggs
- 1/2 C. vegetable oil
- 1 C. milk
- 2 tbsps vanilla extract
- 1/3 C. water
- 2 C. chocolate-hazelnut spread
- 1 C. diced toasted hazelnuts

Directions

1. Coat a muffin tin or 18 muffin C. with oil then set your oven to 350 degrees before doing anything else.
2. Get a bowl, combine: salt, sugar, baking soda, flour, baking powder, ground hazelnut nuts, and cocoa.
3. Get a 2nd bowl, combine, with a mixer, until smooth: vanilla, eggs, milk, and veggie oil.
4. Combine both bowls gradually then add in the water and continue stirring.
5. Evenly divide the mix between your muffin sections.
6. Now cook everything in the oven for 15 mins.
7. Let the muffins cool for 15 mins before topping them with the hazelnut spread.
8. Enjoy.

TRUFFLE and Hazelnut Desserts

Prep Time: 20 mins
Total Time: 45 mins

Servings per Recipe: 24
Calories	345 kcal
Fat	18.9 g
Carbohydrates	39.3g
Protein	5.2 g
Cholesterol	44 mg
Sodium	135 mg

Ingredients

- 2 1/4 C. all-purpose flour
- 1/2 C. unsweetened cocoa powder
- 1 tbsp baking powder
- 3/4 C. milk
- 1/4 C. hazelnut liqueur
- 1 tbsp vanilla extract
- 1 C. butter
- 1 1/2 C. white sugar
- 3 eggs
- 24 chocolate-hazelnut truffles (such as Ferrero Rocher(R))
- 1 (13 oz.) jar chocolate-hazelnut spread
- 1/4 C. diced hazelnuts

Directions

1. Cover your muffin C. or a muffin tin with foil liners or parchment paper and then set your oven to 350 degrees before doing anything else.
2. Get a bowl, sift: baking powder, flour, and cocoa.
3. Get a 2nd bowl, combine: vanilla, liqueur, and milk.
4. Get a 3rd bowl, combine, with a mixer: sugar and butter. Then one by one add in your eggs and continue mixing.
5. As you continue to mix gradually add in your flour mix and the milk mix.
6. Stir the new mix to get everything smooth.
7. Now add about half a C. of mix to each muffin section then put a truffle into each section of batter.
8. Once you have added your unwrapped truffles add more batter.
9. Cook the Cupcakes in the oven for 23 mins then let the cupcakes cool for 15 mins.
10. Coat each dessert with some hazelnut spread.
11. Enjoy.

Pancakes
from Denmark

Prep Time: 5 mins
Total Time: 10 mins

Servings per Recipe: 7
Calories	127 kcal
Fat	4.8 g
Carbohydrates	18g
Protein	4.1 g
Cholesterol	34 mg
Sodium	362 mg

Ingredients

- 1 C. whole wheat flour
- 2 tbsps white sugar
- 2 1/2 tbsps baking powder
- 1/2 tbsp salt
- 1/4 tbsp ground cinnamon
- 1 dash ground nutmeg
- 7 tsps chocolate hazel nut spread
- 1 dash ground cloves
- 1 egg, lightly beaten
- 3/4 C. milk
- 2 tbsps unsalted butter, melted
- 1 tbsp vanilla extract

Directions

1. Get a bowl, combine: cloves, flour, nutmeg, sugar, cinnamon, baking powder, and salt. Then combine in: vanilla, egg, butter, and milk.
2. Get your Aebleskiver pan hot and then coat it with non-stick spray.
3. Ladle the batter into each section and leave about 1/3 of space.
4. Now cook the batter for 4 mins then use a skewer to turn the muffin by ¼ of a turn.
5. Continue this turning process every few mins until everything is cooked.
6. Top each of your muffins with 1 tsp of hazelnut spread before serving.
7. Enjoy.

STRAWBERRY
Hazelnut Bark

Prep Time: 15 mins
Total Time: 1 hr 15 mins

Servings per Recipe: 45
Calories   276 kcal
Fat   17.5 g
Carbohydrates   28.2g
Protein   6.3 g
Cholesterol   0 mg
Sodium   103 mg

Ingredients

3 C. strawberries, stemmed and quartered
4 C. dark chocolate chips, melted
3 C. peanut butter, melted
3 C. chocolate-hazelnut spread, melted

2 C. marshmallow cream (such as Marshmallow Fluff(R)), melted

Directions

1. Cover a cookie sheet with parchment paper.
2. Get a bowl and add in your strawberries.
3. Grab a potato masher and puree the strawberries.
4. Combine in: marshmallow cream, melted chocolate, hazelnut spread, and peanut butter.
5. Now pour this mix onto your cookie sheet.
6. Place the contents in the fridge for 60 mins.
7. Enjoy.

Two Times Chocolate Cookies

Prep Time: 25 mins
Total Time: 40 mins

Servings per Recipe: 24
Calories	133 kcal
Fat	8.3 g
Carbohydrates	14.3g
Protein	1.6 g
Cholesterol	18 mg
Sodium	82 mg

Ingredients

- 1/2 C. butter, at room temperature
- 3/4 C. white sugar
- 1/4 tbsp salt
- 1 egg
- 1 tbsp vanilla extract
- 1 3/4 oz. 70% dark chocolate, melted
- 1 tbsp cocoa powder
- 1/4 tbsp instant espresso powder (optional)
- 1 C. all-purpose flour
- 1/2 C. semisweet chocolate chips
- 1/2 C. roasted hazelnuts, diced
- 1/4 C. roasted hazelnuts, finely ground
- 4 tbsps hazelnut spread

Directions

1. Cover two cookie sheets with parchment paper and then set your oven to 325 degrees before doing anything else.
2. With an electric mixer, mix your butter until fluffy, in a bowl. Then combine in salt and sugar.
3. Continue mixing then add in the vanilla, eggs, expresso, melted chocolate, and cocoa.
4. Mix the contents for 60 secs before adding the flour in slowly.
5. Once the mix is smooth add the ground and diced hazelnuts and also the chocolate chips.
6. Drop dollops of the mix onto the cookie sheets and flatten them with a spoon.
7. Cook the cookies in the oven for 15 mins then let them cool for 10 mins before serving and topping each one with some hazelnut spread.
8. Enjoy.

HAZELNUT
Peanut Butter Sandwiches

Prep Time: 10 mins
Total Time: 15 mins

Servings per Recipe: 6
Calories   416 kcal
Fat   26.1 g
Carbohydrates   38g
Protein   12 g
Cholesterol   0 mg
Sodium   348 mg

Ingredients

6 slices sandwich bread
3/4 C. peanut butter
3/4 C. chocolate-hazelnut spread

Directions

1. Take your pieces of bread, remove the crusts, and then toast them.
2. Coat twelve pieces of bread with peanut butter and then coat the other pieces of bread with the chocolate hazelnut spread.
3. Form a sandwich from one slice with peanut butter and one slice with hazelnut spread.
4. Enjoy.

Nutella Puff Pastry

Prep Time: 5 mins
Total Time: 20 mins

Servings per Recipe: 34
Calories   16 kcal
Carbohydrates   10.2 g
Cholesterol   0 mg
Fat   7.9 g
Protein   1.6 g
Sodium   40 mg

Ingredients

1 (17.25 oz) package frozen puff pastry, thawed
11 tbsps chocolate hazelnut spread
1/2 C. chopped hazelnuts (optional)
6 tsps powdered sugar

Directions

1. Set your oven at 425 degrees F before doing anything else.
2. Spread chocolate hazelnut spread over flattened puff pastry before toping it with hazelnuts.
3. Fold it up into a rectangle shape before cutting it into half inch slices.
4. Put this on a baking dish and sprinkle some powdered sugar.
5. Bake this in the preheated oven for about 15 minutes or until golden brown.
6. Cool it down.
7. Serve.

5 MINUTE
Hazelnut Topped Donut

Prep Time: 5 mins
Total Time: 5 mins

Servings per Recipe: 1
Calories   441.9
Fat   24.6g
Cholesterol   3.6mg
Sodium   220.3mg
Carbohydrates   49.5g
Protein   5.8g

Ingredients

1 doughnut, glazed, halved horizontally
2 tbsp Nutella chocolate hazelnut spread

Directions

1. Place the Nutella onto both cut sides of doughnut halves.
2. Place the top half onto bottom half and enjoy.
3. Enjoy.

Australian Hazelnut Pops

Prep Time: 10 mins
Total Time: 10 mins

Servings per Recipe: 6
Calories   170.6
Fat   9.3 g
Cholesterol   6.1 mg
Sodium   36.3 mg
Carbohydrates   18.2 g
Protein   3.2 g

Ingredients

1/2 C. nutella
1 1/2 C. whole milk
popsicle molds

Dixie paper C.
popsicle stick

Directions

1. In a bowl, add the milk and Nutella and mix until well combined.
2. Transfer the mixture into Popsicle molds and place in the freezer until set completely.
3. Carefully, remove the popsicles from molds and enjoy.

AUSTRALIAN
Hazelnut Crepes

Prep Time: 5 mins
Total Time: 45 mins

Servings per Recipe: 4
Calories 335.8
Fat 15.8g
Cholesterol 114.2mg
Sodium 119.2mg
Carbohydrates 38.0g
Protein 8.7g

Ingredients

1/2 C. all-purpose flour
2 large eggs
1 pinch salt
1 C. milk
1 tsp. orange extract
cooking spray

8 tbsp. nutella
powdered sugar

Directions

1. In a bowl, add the flour, salt, eggs, milk and orange extract and beat until well combined.
2. Lightly grease a crepe pan with the cooking spray and place over medium-high heat until heated through.
3. Place about 1/4 C. of the mixture and tilt the pan to spread in a thin layer.
4. Cook for about 5 minutes, flipping once after 3 minutes.
5. Repeat with the remaining mixture.
6. Place about 1 tbsp. of nutella onto each crepe evenly.
7. Carefully, roll each crepe and enjoy with a dusting of the powder sugar.

Granola
New Zealand

Prep Time: 15 mins
Total Time: 2 hrs 15 mins

Servings per Recipe: 16
Calories	327.6
Fat	15.5g
Cholesterol	0.0mg
Sodium	17.6mg
Carbohydrates	42.0g
Protein	6.5g

Ingredients

- 6 C. rolled oats
- 1/2 C. wheat germ
- 1/4 C. sunflower seeds
- 1/4 C. almonds, chopped
- 1/4 C. raisins
- 1/4 C. craisins
- 1/2 C. brown sugar
- 3/4 C. Nutella
- 1/2 C. canola oil

Directions

1. Before you do anything, preheat the oven to 250 F.
2. Get a mixing bowl: Stir in it the oats with germ, sunflower seeds, and almonds.
3. Place a heavy saucepan over medium heat. Stir in it the brown sugar, Nutella, and oil until the melt.
4. Drizzle them over the oats mixture. Toss them to coat. Spoon the mixture into a lined up baking pan.
5. Bake them for 120 min while stirring them every 20 min.
6. Turn off the heat and stir in the raisins. Allow the granola to lose heat completely then serve it.
7. Enjoy.

AUSTRALIAN
Dream Bars

Prep Time: 5 mins
Total Time: 5 mins

Servings per Recipe: 24
Calories   262.1
Fat   20.5g
Cholesterol   40.6mg
Sodium   141.1mg
Carbohydrates   18.6g
Protein   2.1g

Ingredients

2 C. old-fashioned oats
2 C. creamy peanut butter
1 C. Nutella, spread
1/2 C. honey

1/4 C. ground flax seeds
1/4 C. slivered almonds

Directions

1. Place a heavy saucepan over medium heat. Stir in it the peanut butter and Nutella until they melt.
2. Get a mixing bowl: Combine in it the remaining ingredients. Add the chocolate mix and combine them well.
3. Spoon the mixture to a foil-lined up and greased baking dish. Place it in the fridge for 60 min.
4. Once the time is up, slice it into 24 bars. Serve your granola bars immediately or store it in the fridge until ready to serve.
5. Enjoy.

Chocolate Hazelnut Empanadas

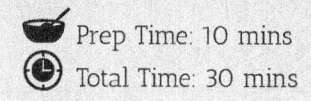

Prep Time: 10 mins
Total Time: 30 mins

Servings per Recipe: 16
Calories 232.3
Fat 13.3g
Cholesterol 0.0mg
Sodium 129.6mg
Carbohydrates 25.7g
Protein 2.5g

Ingredients

1 large ripe banana, peeled and 1/4-inch cubes
1 C. nutella chocolate hazelnut spread
2 refrigerated 9-inch pie shells
2 tbsp. water
2 tbsp. granulated sugar
cinnamon ice cream

Directions

1. In a bowl, add the Nutella and banana and mix until well combined.
2. Place the dough onto a lightly floured surface and cut into 2 equal sized pieces.
3. Now, roll each piece into a 14x8-inch rectangle with 1/4-inch thickness.
4. With a 3-inch cookie cutter, cut 8 circles from each dough rectangle.
5. Place about 1 heaping tsp. of the Nutella mixture onto each dough circle.
6. With wet fingers, moisten the edges of each circle.
7. Fold the dough over the filling and press the edges to seal.
8. In the bottom of a foil lined baking sheet, arrange the empanadas.
9. Coat each empanada with the water and dust with the sugar.
10. Place in the freezer for about 20 minutes.
11. Set your oven to 400 degrees F.
12. Cook in the oven for about 20 minutes.
13. Enjoy warm alongside the cinnamon ice cream.

HAZELNUT Snack Sandwiches

Prep Time: 10 mins
Total Time: 10 mins

Servings per Recipe: 1
Calories   133.2
Fat   4.4g
Cholesterol   0.0mg
Sodium   132.8mg
Carbohydrates   20.3g
Protein   2.5g

Ingredients

12 slices white bread, crusts removed
1/2 C. Nutella
1/2 C. candy sprinkles

Directions

1. Flatten the bread slices using a rolling pin. Place them on a serving plate.
2. Coat one side of them with Nutella. Top them with the candy sprinkles.
3. Roll them tightly and serve them.
4. Enjoy.

Rainbow Sandwiches

Prep Time: 10 mins
Total Time: 30 mins

Servings per Recipe: 32
Calories   111.1
Fat   4.2g
Cholesterol   8.4mg
Sodium   213.2mg
Carbohydrates   15.8g
Protein   2.4g

Ingredients

2 loaves thick-sliced white bread
4.5 oz. unsalted butter, softened
strawberry jam
Nutella
1 C. colored sprinkles
1 C. chocolate sprinkles

Directions

1. Coat one side of one loaf slices with half of the butter.
2. Place them with the buttered side facing down on a cutting board. Top them with jam.
3. Coat one side of the remaining bread slice with butter and the other side with Nutella.
4. Place them over the sandwiches with the buttered side facing up.
5. Slice the sandwiches into triangles.
6. Coat them half of them with chocolate sprinkles and the other half with colored sprinkles.
7. Serve your sandwiches immediately with some milk.
8. Enjoy.

ZARA'S SWEET
Sweet Wontons

Prep Time: 15 mins
Total Time: 30 mins

Servings per Recipe: 6
Calories   104.0
Fat   1.9g
Cholesterol   1.5mg
Sodium   111.1mg
Carbohydrates   19.5g
Protein   2.3g

Ingredients

1 small ripe banana, mashed
1 tbsp nutella
1 tbsp strawberry jam
1 tbsp chopped nuts
13 wonton wrappers
1/2 tsp sugar
nonstick cooking spray

Directions

1. Set your oven to 350 degrees F before doing anything else and line a baking sheet with the parchment paper.
2. In a bowl, add the jam, nutella and banana and the jam and mix until smooth.
3. Place about 1 tsp of the mixture in the center of each wonton wrapper, followed by the nuts.
4. With wet fingers, moisten the edges of each wrapper and then, fold over the filling in a triangle shape.
5. Now, with your fingers, press the edges to seal completely.
6. In a deep skillet, add the oil over medium-high heat and cook until heated through.
7. In the bottom of the prepared baking sheet, arrange the wonton wrappers.
8. Spray each wrapper with the cooking spray and dust with the sugar.
9. Cook in the oven for about 30 minutes 11-15 minutes.
10. Enjoy hot with your favorite topping.

Sweet Wontons
New Zealand

Prep Time: 20 mins
Total Time: 30 mins

Servings per Recipe: 8
Calories	161.3
Fat	6.6g
Cholesterol	9.0mg
Sodium	96.9mg
Carbohydrates	23.4g
Protein	2.4g

Ingredients

- 2 tbsp sugar
- 2 tsp cinnamon
- 16 wonton wrappers
- 5 tbsp nutella
- 1 banana, ripe, sliced
- 2 tbsp unsalted butter

Directions

1. Set your oven to 350 degrees F before doing anything else and line a baking sheet with the parchment paper.
2. In a bowl, add the cinnamon and sugar and mix well.
3. Arrange the wonton wrappers onto a smooth surface.
4. Place 1 tsp of the Nutella in the center of each wrapper, followed by 2 banana slices.
5. With wet fingers, moisten the edges of each wrapper and then, fold over the filling in a triangle shape.
6. Now, with your fingers, press the edges to seal completely.
7. In the bottom of the prepared baking sheet, arrange the wontons.
8. Coat each wonton with the melted butter and dust with the cinnamon sugar.
9. Cook in the oven for about 8-10 minutes.
10. Enjoy warm.

FRENCH
Hazelnut and Chocolate Sandwich Cookies

Prep Time: 25 mins
Total Time: 37 mins

Servings per Recipe: 18
Calories   118.0
Fat   5.2g
Cholesterol   11.5mg
Sodium   99.3mg
Carbohydrates   15.4g
Protein   1.9g

Ingredients

1 C. Nutella
1 extra-large egg
1 C. self-rising cake flour

Directions

1. Set your oven to 375 degrees F before doing anything else and line a baking sheet with the parchment paper.
2. In a bowl, add the egg and 1/2 C. of the Nutella and with an electric mixer, beat until blended nicely.
3. Gradually, add 1 C. of flour, beating until a wet dough forms.
4. Place the dough onto a floured surface and with your hands, gently knead until a sticky dough forms.
5. With floured hands, make 18 equal sized balls from the dough.
6. In the bottom of the prepared baking sheet, arrange the dough balls about 2-3-inch apart.
7. With your fingers, press each ball very slightly.
8. Cook in the oven for about 12 minutes.
9. Remove from the oven and keep onto the wire rack to cool in the pan for about 10 minutes.
10. With a sharp, serrated knife, slice the cookies in half horizontally.
11. Place about 1 tsp of the Nutella onto each bottom half of cookies.
12. Cover with the top halves and press Strongly.
13. Keep onto the wire rack to cool completely.
14. Enjoy.
15. You can store these cookies in an airtight jar.

Pavlova II

🥣 Prep Time: 30 mins
🕐 Total Time: 2 hrs

Servings per Recipe: 8
Calories   316.9
Fat   18.0g
Cholesterol   61.1mg
Sodium   51.4mg
Carbohydrates   37.0g
Protein   2.8g

Ingredients

Meringue
3 egg whites, room temperature
1 pinch cream of tartar
3/4 C. granulated sugar
1 tsp pure vanilla extract
Cream
1/2 C. marshmallow crème
1/2 C. crème fraiche
1 C. whipping cream
Garnishing
1 kiwi fruit, peeled & sliced thinly
1 C. sliced strawberry
2 tbsp dried cranberries, minced
2 tbsp Nutella

Directions

1. Set your oven to 275 degrees F before doing anything else and line a baking sheet with the parchment paper.
2. In a bowl, add the egg whites and cream of tartar and beat till soft peaks form, adding the sugar 1 tbsp at a time.
3. Add the vanilla and beat to combine.
4. Onto the prepared baking sheet, spread the meringue into a 10-inch circle, pushing up edges to form a well in the middle.
5. Cook in the oven for about 1 1/2 hours.
6. Turn off the oven but leave the meringue inside to dry.
7. Transfer the meringue into a serving platter.
8. In a bowl, mix together the marshmallow crème and crème fraiche.
9. Fold in the whipped cream.
10. Spread the marshmallow mixture over the cooled meringue and decorate with the sliced kiwi and strawberries.
11. Drizzle the Nutella on top and serve with a sprinkling of the dried cranberries.

DESSERT
Wontons

Prep Time: 15 mins
Total Time: 30 mins

Servings per Recipe: 1
Calories   32.8
Fat   0.1g
Cholesterol   0.6mg
Sodium   40.7mg
Carbohydrates   7.2g
Protein   0.8g

Ingredients

Nutella, as required
2 large ripe bananas, peeled and cut into 1/2 inch thick slices
coconut flakes, as required
6 oz. wonton wrappers, about 24
1 tbsp light brown sugar

1/4 tsp ground cinnamon
pinch of ground nutmeg
pinch of ground cardamom
oil (for frying)
powdered sugar

Directions

1. In a bowl, mix together the brown sugar and spices.
2. Add the banana slices and coat them with the brown sugar mixture evenly.
3. Place a small amount of nutella, followed by a banana slice and some piece of coconut flakes in the center of each wonton wrapper.
4. Coat the edges of the wrappers with wet fingers and fold them over the filling in a triangle shape.
5. With your fingers, press the edges to seal them completely.
6. In a large skillet heat the oil to 350 degrees F.
7. Add the wontons in batches and cook till golden brown on both sides.
8. Transfer the wrappers onto a paper towel lined plate to drain.
9. Serve everything with a sprinkling of powdered sugar.

Nutella Truffles

Prep Time: 25 mins
Total Time: 12 hrs 40 mins

Servings per Recipe: 28
Calories   135 kcal
Fat   8 g
Carbohydrates   16.9 g
Protein   1.6 g
Cholesterol   8 mg
Sodium   219 mg

Ingredients

- 1 C. chocolate-hazelnut spread
- 1/3 C. white sugar
- 2 tbsp water
- 2/3 C. heavy whipping cream
- 1/4 tsp coarse sea salt
- 1/2 C. unsweetened cocoa powder
- 1 (12 oz.) bag chocolate chips (at least cocoa), finely chopped
- 1 tbsp coarse sea salt (such as Diamond Crystal(R)), or to taste

Directions

1. Add the hazelnut spread in metal bowl over a pan of gently simmering water and stir till the hazelnut spread is warm and smooth for about 5 minutes.
2. Remove the bowl from the heat.
3. In a small pan, add the sugar and water on medium heat and stir till dissolved.
4. Brush the sides of the pan with a moistened pastry brush occasionally as the sugar mixture cooks.
5. Increase the heat to medium-high and bring syrup to a boil and cook for about 4 minutes, brushing down sides and swirling the pan occasionally to prevent scorching.
6. Add the cream into the syrup, stirring continuously.
7. Reduce the heat to low and cook, stirring continuously for about 5-10 minutes.
8. Gently stir in 1/4 tsp of salt into the melted hazelnut spread.
9. Refrigerate caramel mixture for at least 3 hours.
10. In a shallow dish, place the cocoa powder.
11. With about 1 tbsp of the mixture, make the balls and coat with the cocoa powder.
12. Arrange the balls onto a baking sheet.
13. With a plastic wrap, cover truffle balls and refrigerate to chill for about 8 hours.
14. Line a 13x9-inch baking sheet with foil.

15. Heat chopped chocolate in a metal bowl set over a saucepan of gently simmering water, stirring frequently until chocolate is melted and smooth.
16. Remove the bowl from the pan of water.
17. Working quickly, dip each truffle ball in the melted chocolate.
18. With a fork, lift the truffles from the chocolate and tap fork against side of bowl to remove excess coating.
19. Transfer the truffles to foil-lined pan to cool.
20. Sprinkle the finished truffles lightly with 1 tbsp of the coarse sea salt before the chocolate hardens.
21. Keep aside for at least 1 hour before serving.

Kid's Favorite Strawberries

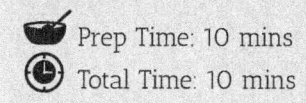

Prep Time: 10 mins
Total Time: 10 mins

Servings per Recipe: 6
Calories 111.6
Fat 5.6g
Cholesterol 0.0mg
Sodium 7.9mg
Carbohydrates 14.2g
Protein 1.2g

Ingredients

18 strawberries
18 tsp Nutella

Directions

1. Wash the strawberries and with the paper towels pat dry.
2. Hull the strawberries and remove the center stem.
3. Place about 1 tsp of the Nutella into each strawberry and serve.

ENJOY THE RECIPES?

KEEP ON COOKING
WITH 6 MORE FREE COOKBOOKS!

Visit our website and simply enter your email address to join the club and receive your 6 cookbooks.

http://booksumo.com/magnet

https://www.instagram.com/booksumopress/

https://www.facebook.com/booksumo/

Printed in Great Britain
by Amazon